my mom
who
always
pushes me
to dream.

DATE:

Today's **MOOD is:** 😐 🙂 😊 😖 😭 😔 😣

i am:
- ◯
- ◯
- ◯

My 6 Self Care Moments:

Breakfast:

Lunch:

Dinner:

Be PROUD, Be BOLD, Don't be afraid to BLOOM

Energy Level: 1 2 3 4 5 6 7 8 9 10

Hydration Tracker:

Exercise

Today's physical Activity:

Minutes:

NOTES

This Weeks Affirmations:

Tomorrow's Focus

Beginning of Day
Thoughts

Time:

End of Day
Thoughts

Time:

DATE:

Today's **MOOD is:** 😐 🙂 😄 😖 😭 😞 😣

i am:
- ○
- ○
- ○

My 6 Self Care Moments:

Breakfast:

Lunch:

Dinner:

Be PROUD, Be BOLD, Don't be afraid to BLOOM

Energy Level: 1 2 3 4 5 6 7 8 9 10

Hydration Tracker:

Exercise

Today's physical Activity:

Minutes:

NOTES

This Weeks Affirmations:

Tomorrow's Focus

Beginning of Day
Thoughts

Time:

End of Day

Thoughts

Time:

DATE:

Today's **MOOD is:** 😐 🙂 😄 😖 😭 😒 😨

i am:
- ○
- ○
- ○

My 6 Self Care Moments:

Breakfast:

Lunch:

Dinner:

Be PROUD, Be BOLD, Don't be afraid to BLOOM

Energy Level: 1 2 3 4 5 6 7 8 9 10

Hydration Tracker:

Exercise

Today's physical Activity:

Minutes:

NOTES

This Weeks Affirmations:

Tomorrow's Focus

Beginning of Day
Thoughts

Time:

End of Day

Thoughts

Time:

DATE:

Today's **MOOD is:** 😐 😊 😊 😖 😭 😟 😫

i am:
- ○
- ○
- ○

My 6 Self Care Moments:

Breakfast:

Lunch:

Dinner:

Be PROUD, Be BOLD, Don't be afraid to BLOOM

Energy Level: 1 2 3 4 5 6 7 8 9 10

Hydration Tracker:

○ ○ ○ ○ ○ ○ ○ ○

Exercise

Today's physical Activity:

Minutes:

NOTES

This Weeks Affirmations:

Tomorrow's Focus

Beginning of Day
Thoughts

Time:

End of Day

Thoughts

Time:

DATE:

Today's **MOOD is:** 😐 🙂 😊 😖 😭 😟 😧

i am:
○
○
○

My 6 Self Care Moments:

Breakfast:

Lunch:

Dinner:

Be PROUD, Be BOLD, Don't be afraid to BLOOM

Energy Level: 1 2 3 4 5 6 7 8 9 10

Hydration Tracker:

○ ○ ○ ○ ○ ○ ○ ○

Exercise

Today's physical Activity:

Minutes:

NOTES

This Weeks Affirmations:

Tomorrow's Focus

○

○

○

Beginning of Day
Thoughts

Time:

End of Day

Thoughts

Time:

DATE:

Today's **MOOD is:** 😐 🙂 😊 😖 😭 😣 😧

i am:
- ◯
- ◯
- ◯

My 6 Self Care Moments:

Breakfast:

Lunch:

Dinner:

Be PROUD, Be BOLD, Don't be afraid to BLOOM

Energy Level: 1 2 3 4 5 6 7 8 9 10

Hydration Tracker:

Exercise

Today's physical Activity:

Minutes:

NOTES

This Weeks Affirmations:

Tomorrow's Focus

Beginning of Day
Thoughts

Time:

End of Day
Thoughts

Time:

DATE:

Today's **MOOD is:** 😐 🙂 😊 😖 😭 😒 😩

i am:
○
○
○

My 6 Self Care Moments:

Breakfast:

Lunch:

Dinner:

Be PROUD, Be BOLD, Don't be afraid to BLOOM

Energy Level: 1 2 3 4 5 6 7 8 9 10

Hydration Tracker:

Exercise

Today's physical Activity:

Minutes:

NOTES

This Weeks Affirmations:

Tomorrow's Focus

○
○
○

Beginning of Day
Thoughts

Time:

End of Day

Thoughts

Time:

DATE:

Today's **MOOD is:** 😐 🙂 😊 😖 😭 😩 😫

i am:
- ○
- ○
- ○

My 6 Self Care Moments:

Breakfast:

Lunch:

Dinner:

Be PROUD, Be BOLD, Don't be afraid to BLOOM

Energy Level: 1 2 3 4 5 6 7 8 9 10

Hydration Tracker:

Exercise

Today's physical Activity:

Minutes:

NOTES

This Weeks Affirmations:

Tomorrow's Focus

○
○
○

… BEGINNING OF DAY
Thoughts

Time:

End of Day
Thoughts

Time:

DATE:

Today's **MOOD is:** 😐 🙂 😄 😖 😭 😩 😫

i am:
-
-
-

My 6 Self Care Moments:

Breakfast:

Lunch:

Dinner:

Be PROUD, Be BOLD, Don't be afraid to BLOOM

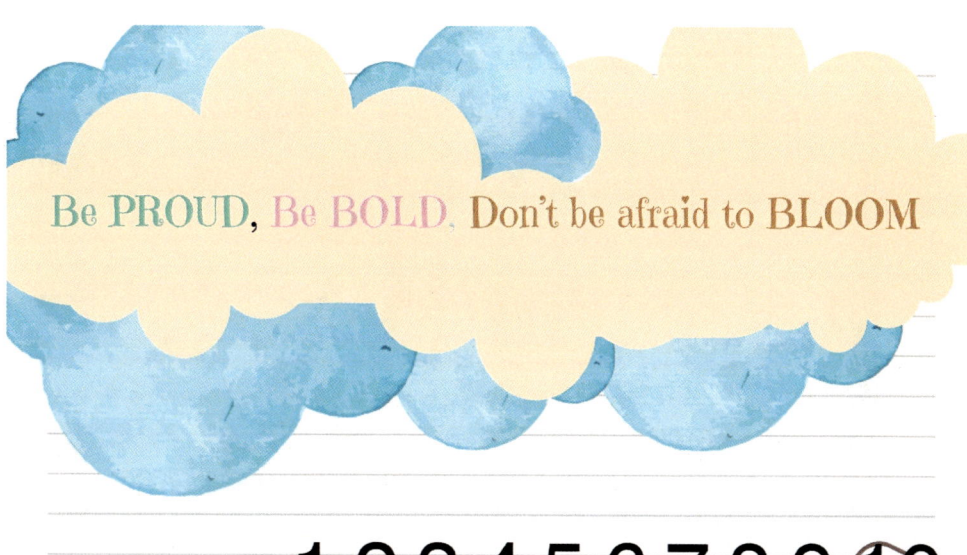

Energy Level: 1 2 3 4 5 6 7 8 9 10

Hydration Tracker:

○ ○ ○ ○ ○ ○ ○ ○

Exercise

Today's physical Activity:

Minutes:

NOTES

This Weeks Affirmations:

Tomorrow's Focus

Beginning of Day
Thoughts

Time:

End of day

Thoughts

Time:

DATE:

Today's **MOOD is:** 😐 🙂 😊 😖 😭 😫 😣

i am:
- ○
- ○
- ○

My 6 Self Care Moments:

Breakfast:

Lunch:

Dinner:

Be PROUD, Be BOLD. Don't be afraid to BLOOM

Energy Level: 1 2 3 4 5 6 7 8 9 10

Hydration Tracker:

Exercise

Today's physical Activity:

Minutes:

NOTES

This Weeks Affirmations:

Tomorrow's Focus

○
○
○

Beginning of Day
Thoughts

Time:

End of day
Thoughts

Time:

DATE:

Today's **MOOD is:** 😐 🙂 😊 😖 😭 😟 😢

i am:
- ○
- ○
- ○

My 6 Self Care Moments:

Breakfast:

Lunch:

Dinner:

Be PROUD, Be BOLD. Don't be afraid to BLOOM

Energy Level: 1 2 3 4 5 6 7 8 9 10

Hydration Tracker:

Exercise

Today's physical Activity:

Minutes:

NOTES

This Weeks Affirmations:

Tomorrow's Focus

○
○
○

Beginning of Day
Thoughts

Time:

End of Day

Thoughts

Time:

DATE:

Today's **MOOD** is: 😐 🙂 😆 😖 😭 😒 😣

i am:
- ○
- ○
- ○

My 6 Self Care Moments:

Breakfast:

Lunch:

Dinner:

Be PROUD, Be BOLD, Don't be afraid to BLOOM

Energy Level: 1 2 3 4 5 6 7 8 9 10

Hydration Tracker:

Exercise

Today's physical Activity:

Minutes:

NOTES

This Weeks Affirmations:

Tomorrow's Focus

Beginning of Day
Thoughts

Time:

End of Day

Thoughts

Time:

DATE:

Today's **MOOD is:** 😐 🙂 😊 😖 😭 😣 😫

i am:
- ○
- ○
- ○

My 6 Self Care Moments:

Breakfast:

Lunch:

Dinner:

Be PROUD, Be BOLD, Don't be afraid to BLOOM

Energy Level: 1 2 3 4 5 6 7 8 9 10

Hydration Tracker:

Exercise

Today's physical Activity:

Minutes:

NOTES

This Weeks Affirmations:

Tomorrow's Focus

○
○
○

Beginning of Day
Thoughts

Time:

End of Day
Thoughts

Time:

DATE:

Today's **MOOD is:** 😐 🙂 😄 😖 😭 😪 😨

i am:
- ○
- ○
- ○

My 6 Self Care Moments:

Breakfast:

Lunch:

Dinner:

Be PROUD, Be BOLD. Don't be afraid to BLOOM

Energy Level: 1 2 3 4 5 6 7 8 9 10

Hydration Tracker:

Exercise

Today's physical Activity:

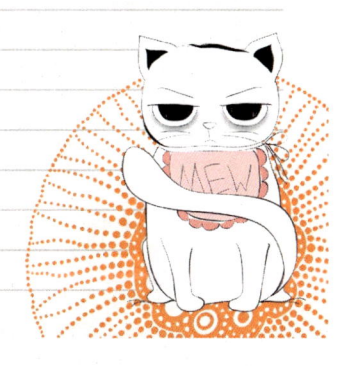

Minutes:

NOTES

This Weeks Affirmations:

Tomorrow's Focus

DATE:

Today's **MOOD is:** 😐 🙂 😊 😖 😭 😩 😞

i am:
- ○
- ○
- ○

My 6 Self Care Moments:

Breakfast:

Lunch:

Dinner:

Be PROUD, Be BOLD, Don't be afraid to BLOOM

Energy Level: 1 2 3 4 5 6 7 8 9 10

Hydration Tracker:

Exercise

Today's physical Activity:

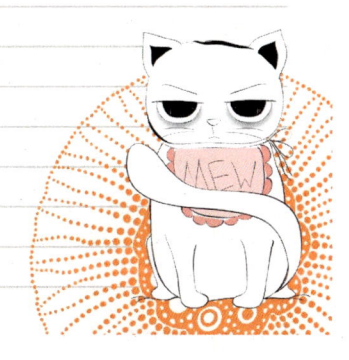

Minutes:

NOTES

This Weeks Affirmations:

Tomorrow's Focus

Beginning of Day
Thoughts

Time:

End of Day

Thoughts

Time:

DATE:

Today's MOOD is: 😐 🙂 😆 😖 😭 😞 😣

i am:
○
○
○

My 6 Self Care Moments:

Breakfast:

Lunch:

Dinner:

Be PROUD, Be BOLD, Don't be afraid to BLOOM

Energy Level: 1 2 3 4 5 6 7 8 9 10

Hydration Tracker:

Exercise

Today's physical Activity:

Minutes:

NOTES

This Weeks Affirmations:

Tomorrow's Focus

Beginning of Day
Thoughts

Time:

End of Day

Thoughts

Time:

DATE:

Today's **MOOD is:** 😐 🙂 😄 😖 😭 😔 😣

i am:
- ◯
- ◯
- ◯

My 6 Self Care Moments:

Breakfast:

Lunch:

Dinner:

Be PROUD, Be BOLD, Don't be afraid to BLOOM

Energy Level: 1 2 3 4 5 6 7 8 9 10

Hydration Tracker:

Exercise

Today's physical Activity:

Minutes:

NOTES

This Weeks Affirmations:

Tomorrow's Focus

○

○

○

Beginning of Day
Thoughts

Time:

End of Day

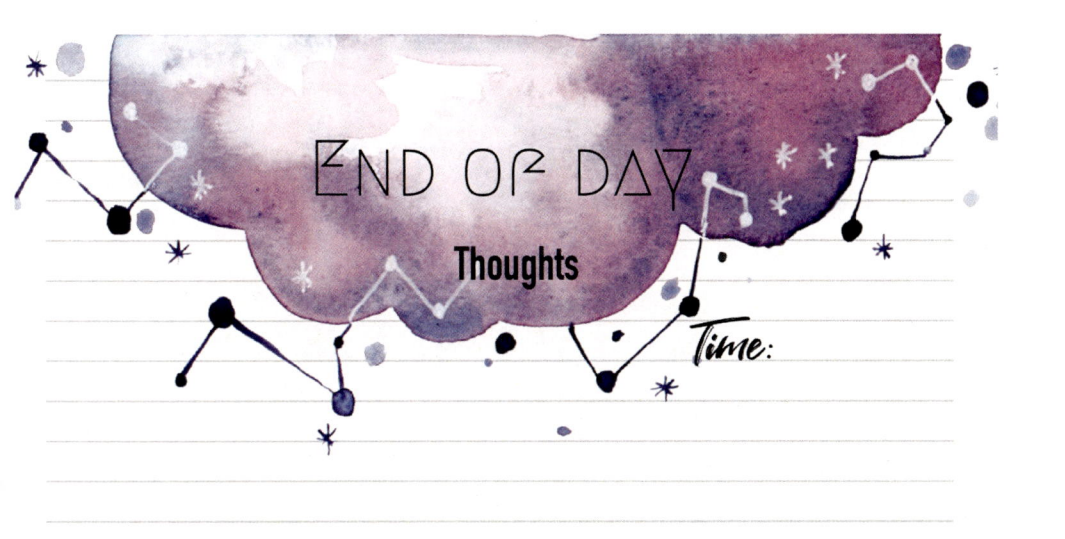

Thoughts

Time:

DATE:

Today's MOOD is: 😐 🙂 😊 😖 😭 😫 ☹️

i am:
○
○
○

My 6 Self Care Moments:

Breakfast:

Lunch:

Dinner:

Be PROUD, Be BOLD, Don't be afraid to BLOOM

Energy Level: 1 2 3 4 5 6 7 8 9 10

Hydration Tracker:

Exercise

Today's physical Activity:

Minutes:

NOTES

This Weeks Affirmations:

Tomorrow's Focus

○

○

○

Beginning of Day
Thoughts

Time:

End of Day
Thoughts

Time:

DATE:

Today's **MOOD is:** 😐 🙂 😆 😖 😭 😣 😫

i am:
- ○
- ○
- ○

My 6 Self Care Moments:

Breakfast:

Lunch:

Dinner:

Be PROUD, Be BOLD. Don't be afraid to BLOOM

Energy Level: 1 2 3 4 5 6 7 8 9 10

Hydration Tracker:

Exercise

Today's physical Activity:

Minutes:

NOTES

This Weeks Affirmations:

Tomorrow's Focus

○
○
○

Beginning of Day
Thoughts

Time:

End of Day

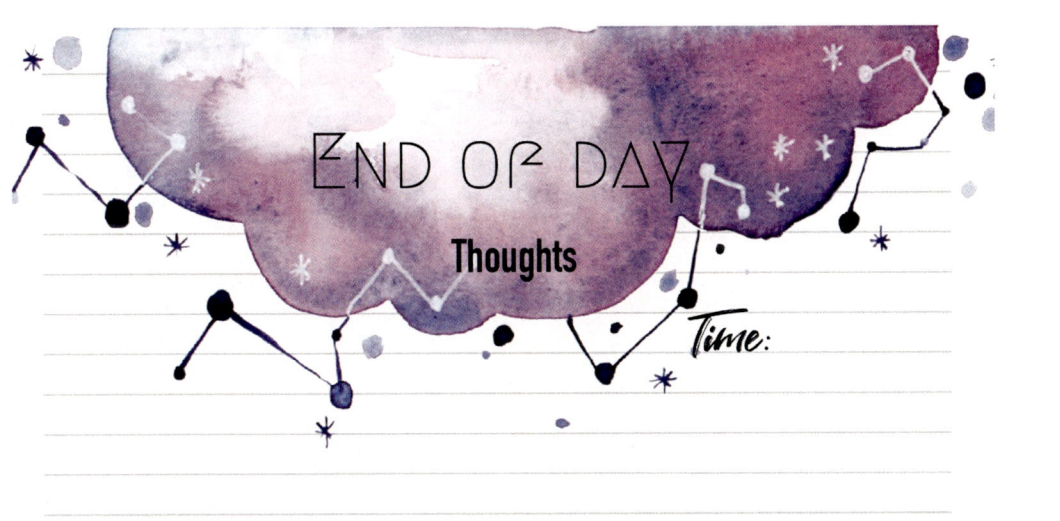

Thoughts

Time:

DATE:

Today's **MOOD is:** 😐 🙂 😊 😖 😭 😟 😣

i am:
○
○
○

My 6 Self Care Moments:

Breakfast:

Lunch:

Dinner:

Be PROUD, Be BOLD, Don't be afraid to BLOOM

Energy Level: 1 2 3 4 5 6 7 8 9 10

Hydration Tracker:

Exercise

Today's physical Activity:

Minutes:

NOTES

This Weeks Affirmations:

Tomorrow's Focus

○

○

○

Beginning of Day
Thoughts

Time:

End of Day

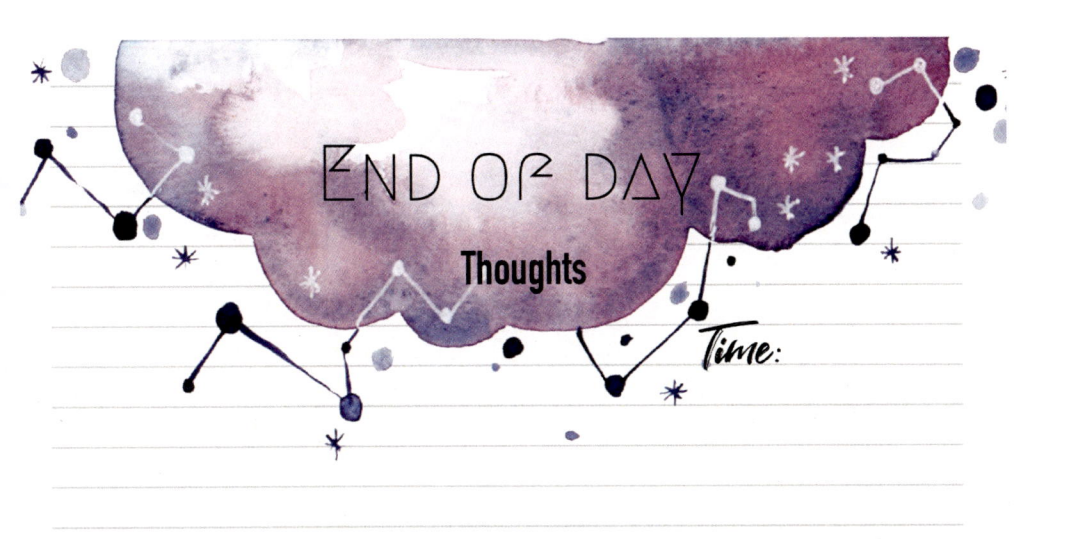

Thoughts

Time:

DATE:

Today's **MOOD is:** 😐 🙂 😊 😖 😭 😒 😞

i am:
- ◯
- ◯
- ◯

My 6 Self Care Moments:

Breakfast:

Lunch:

Dinner:

Be PROUD, Be BOLD, Don't be afraid to BLOOM

Energy Level: 1 2 3 4 5 6 7 8 9 10

Hydration Tracker:

Exercise

Today's physical Activity:

Minutes:

NOTES

This Weeks Affirmations:

Tomorrow's Focus

○
○
○

Beginning of Day
Thoughts

Time:

End of Day

Thoughts

Time:

DATE:

Today's **MOOD is:** 😐 🙂 😊 😖 😭 😔 😩

i am:
- ○
- ○
- ○

My 6 Self Care Moments:

Breakfast:

Lunch:

Dinner:

Be PROUD, Be BOLD. Don't be afraid to BLOOM

Energy Level: 1 2 3 4 5 6 7 8 9 10

Hydration Tracker:

○ ○ ○ ○ ○ ○ ○ ○

Exercise

Today's physical Activity:

Minutes:

NOTES

This Weeks Affirmations:

Tomorrow's Focus

Beginning of Day
Thoughts

Time:

End of Day

Thoughts

Time:

DATE:

Today's MOOD is: 😐 😊 😄 😖 😭 😒 😣

i am:
- ○
- ○
- ○

My 6 Self Care Moments:

Breakfast:

Lunch:

Dinner:

Be PROUD, Be BOLD, Don't be afraid to BLOOM

Energy Level: 1 2 3 4 5 6 7 8 9 10

Hydration Tracker:

Exercise

Today's physical Activity:

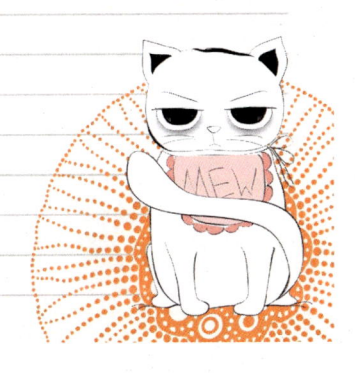

Minutes:

NOTES

This Weeks Affirmations:

Tomorrow's Focus

Beginning of Day
Thoughts

Time:

End of Day

Thoughts

Time:

DATE:

Today's **MOOD is:** 😐 🙂 😄 😖 😭 😒 😣

i am:
○
○
○

My 6 Self Care Moments:

Breakfast:

Lunch:

Dinner:

Be PROUD, Be BOLD. Don't be afraid to BLOOM

Energy Level: 1 2 3 4 5 6 7 8 9 10

Hydration Tracker:

Exercise

Today's physical Activity:

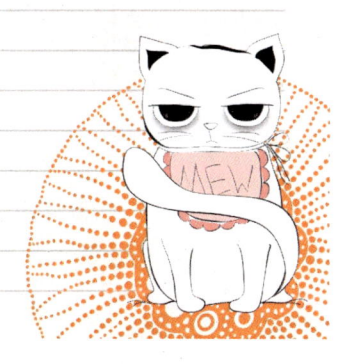

Minutes:

NOTES

This Weeks Affirmations:

Tomorrow's Focus

Beginning of Day
Thoughts

Time:

End of Day

Thoughts

Time:

DATE:

Today's **MOOD is:**

i am:
-
-
-

My 6 Self Care Moments:

Breakfast:

Lunch:

Dinner:

Be PROUD, Be BOLD, Don't be afraid to BLOOM

Energy Level: 1 2 3 4 5 6 7 8 9 10

Hydration Tracker:

Exercise

Today's physical Activity:

Minutes:

NOTES

This Weeks Affirmations:

Tomorrow's Focus

○

○

○

Beginning of Day
Thoughts

Time:

End of Day

Thoughts

Time:

DATE:

Today's **MOOD** is: 😐 🙂 😊 😖 😭 😩 😟

i am:
- ○
- ○
- ○

My 6 Self Care Moments:

Breakfast:

Lunch:

Dinner:

Be PROUD, Be BOLD, Don't be afraid to BLOOM

Energy Level: 1 2 3 4 5 6 7 8 9 10

Hydration Tracker:

Exercise

Today's physical Activity:

Minutes:

NOTES

This Weeks Affirmations:

Tomorrow's Focus

○
○
○

Beginning of Day
Thoughts

Time:

End of Day

Thoughts

Time:

DATE:

Today's **MOOD is:** 😐 🙂 😄 😖 😭 😒 😫

i am:
- ◯
- ◯
- ◯

My 6 Self Care Moments:

Breakfast:

Lunch:

Dinner:

Be PROUD, Be BOLD, Don't be afraid to BLOOM

Energy Level: 1 2 3 4 5 6 7 8 9 10

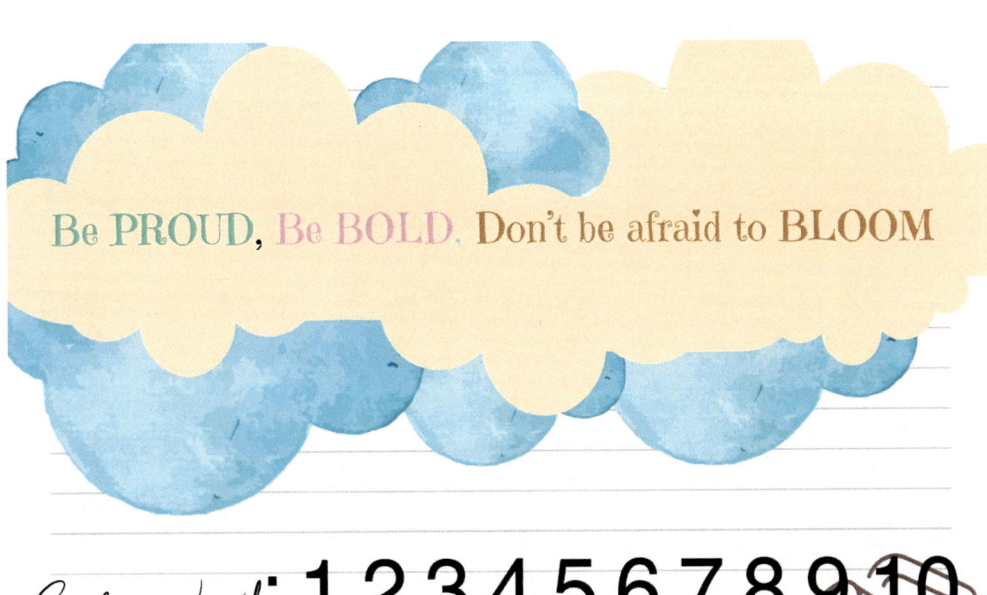

Hydration Tracker:

Exercise

Today's physical Activity:

Minutes:

NOTES

This Weeks Affirmations:

Tomorrow's Focus

Beginning of Day
Thoughts

Time:

… End of Day

Thoughts

Time:

DATE:

Today's **MOOD** is: 😐 🙂 😊 😖 😭 😒 😩

i am:
○
○
○

My 6 Self Care Moments:

Breakfast:

Lunch:

Dinner:

Be PROUD, Be BOLD, Don't be afraid to BLOOM

Energy Level: 1 2 3 4 5 6 7 8 9 10

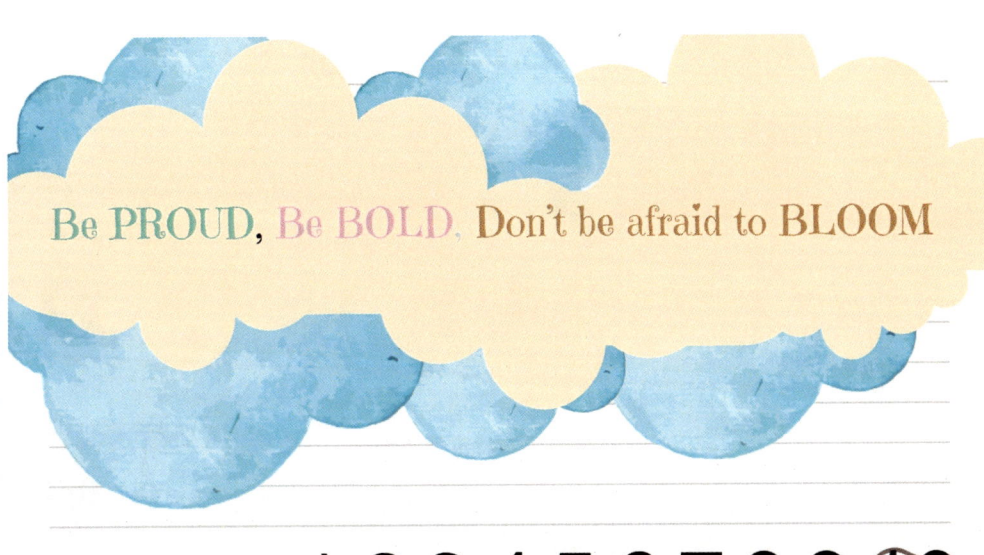

Hydration Tracker:

Exercise

Today's physical Activity:

Minutes:

NOTES

This Weeks Affirmations:

Tomorrow's Focus

End of Day

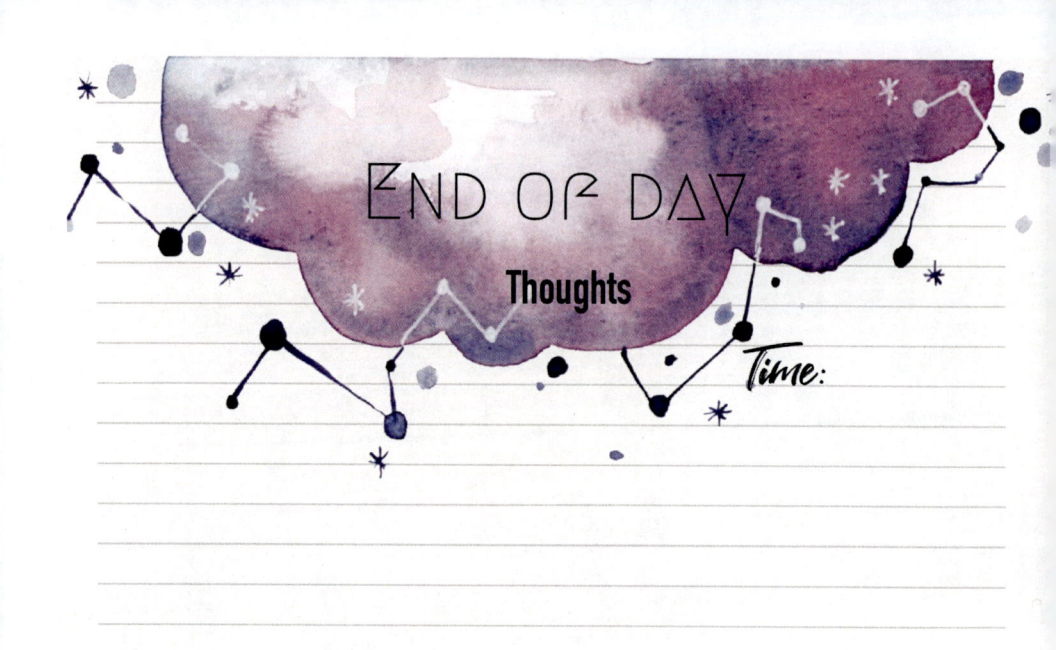

Thoughts

Time:

Beginning of Day
Thoughts

Time:

DATE:

Today's MOOD is: 🙂 😊 😄 😖 😭 😣 😞

i am:
○
○
○

My 6 Self Care Moments:

Breakfast:

Lunch:

Dinner:

Be PROUD, Be BOLD. Don't be afraid to BLOOM

Energy Level: 1 2 3 4 5 6 7 8 9 10

Hydration Tracker:

Exercise

Today's physical Activity:

Minutes:

NOTES

This Weeks Affirmations:

Tomorrow's Focus

Beginning of Day
Thoughts

Time:

End of Day

Thoughts

Time:

DATE:

Today's **MOOD is:** 😐 🙂 😊 😖 😭 😞 ☹️

i am:
- ○
- ○
- ○

My 6 Self Care Moments:

Breakfast:

Lunch:

Dinner:

Be PROUD, Be BOLD, Don't be afraid to BLOOM

Energy Level: 1 2 3 4 5 6 7 8 9 10

Hydration Tracker:

Exercise

Today's physical Activity:

Minutes:

NOTES

This Weeks Affirmations:

Tomorrow's Focus

○

○

○

Beginning of Day
Thoughts

Time:

End of Day
Thoughts

Time:

DATE:

Today's **MOOD is:** 😐 🙂 😄 😖 😭 😩 😞

i am:
- ○
- ○
- ○

My 6 Self Care Moments:

Breakfast:

Lunch:

Dinner:

Be PROUD, Be BOLD. Don't be afraid to BLOOM

Energy Level: 1 2 3 4 5 6 7 8 9 10

Hydration Tracker:

Exercise

Today's physical Activity:

Minutes:

NOTES

This Weeks Affirmations:

Tomorrow's Focus

○
○
○

Beginning of Day
Thoughts

Time:

End of Day

Thoughts

Time:

DATE:

Today's **MOOD** is: 😐 🙂 😊 😖 😭 😒 😫

i am:
○
○
○

My 6 Self Care Moments:

Breakfast:

Lunch:

Dinner:

Be PROUD, Be BOLD. Don't be afraid to BLOOM

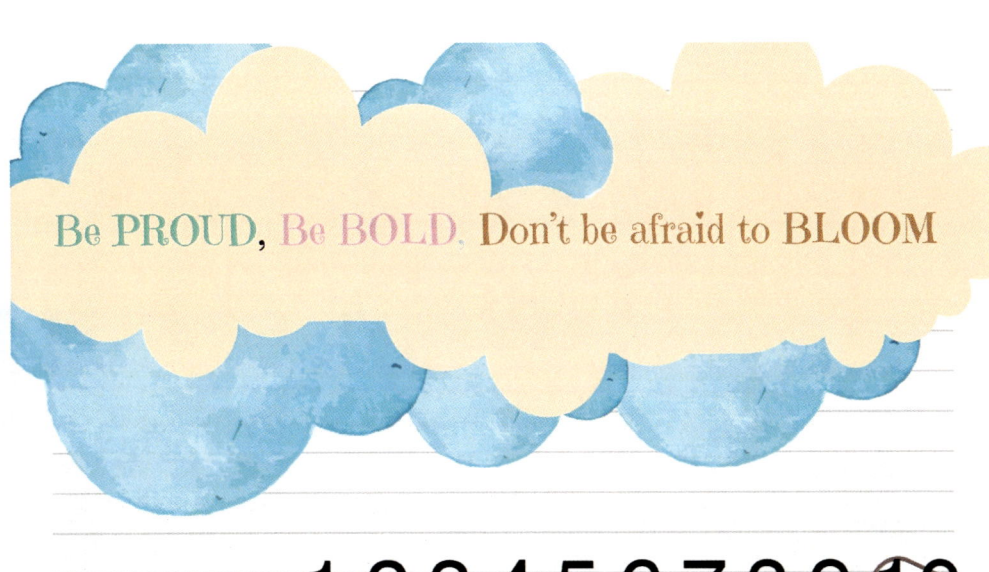

Energy Level: 1 2 3 4 5 6 7 8 9 10

Hydration Tracker:

Exercise

Today's physical Activity:

Minutes:

NOTES

This Weeks Affirmations:

Tomorrow's Focus

Beginning of Day
Thoughts

Time:

End of Day

Thoughts

Time:

DATE:

Today's **MOOD is:** 😐 🙂 😄 😖 😭 😩 😞

i am:
- ○
- ○
- ○

My 6 Self Care Moments:

Breakfast:

Lunch:

Dinner:

Be PROUD, Be BOLD, Don't be afraid to BLOOM

Energy Level: 1 2 3 4 5 6 7 8 9 10

Hydration Tracker:

Exercise

Today's physical Activity:

Minutes:

NOTES

This Weeks Affirmations:

Tomorrow's Focus

○

○

○

Beginning of Day
Thoughts

Time:

End of Day

Thoughts

Time:

DATE:

Today's **MOOD is:** 😐 😊 😄 😣 😭 😩 😫

i am:
○
○
○

My 6 Self Care Moments:

Breakfast:

Lunch:

Dinner:

Be PROUD, Be BOLD, Don't be afraid to BLOOM

Energy Level: 1 2 3 4 5 6 7 8 9 10

Hydration Tracker:

Exercise

Today's physical Activity:

Minutes:

NOTES

This Weeks Affirmations:

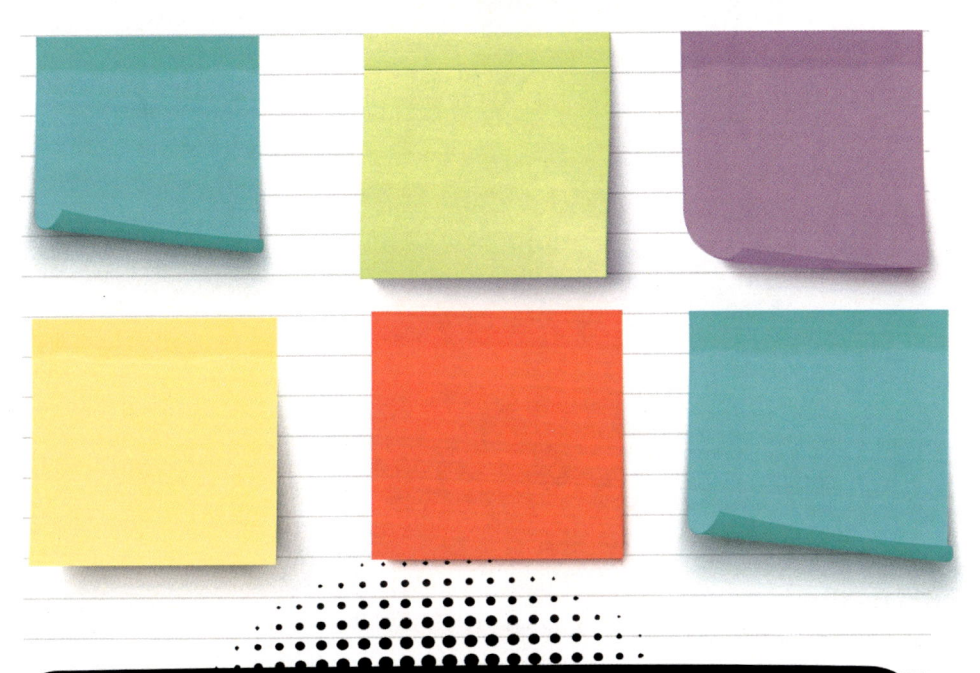

Tomorrow's Focus

Beginning of Day
Thoughts

Time:

End of Day
Thoughts

Time:

DATE:

Today's **MOOD is:** 😐 🙂 😊 😖 😭 😒 😫

i am:
- ○
- ○
- ○

My 6 Self Care Moments:

Breakfast:

Lunch:

Dinner:

Be PROUD, Be BOLD. Don't be afraid to BLOOM

Energy Level: 1 2 3 4 5 6 7 8 9 10

Hydration Tracker:

Exercise

Today's physical Activity:

Minutes:

NOTES

This Weeks Affirmations:

Tomorrow's Focus

○

○

○

Beginning of Day
Thoughts

Time:

End of Day

Thoughts

Time:

DATE:

Today's **MOOD is:** 😐 🙂 😊 😖 😭 😔 😞

i am:
- ○
- ○
- ○

My 6 Self Care Moments:

Breakfast:

Lunch:

Dinner:

Be PROUD, Be BOLD, Don't be afraid to BLOOM

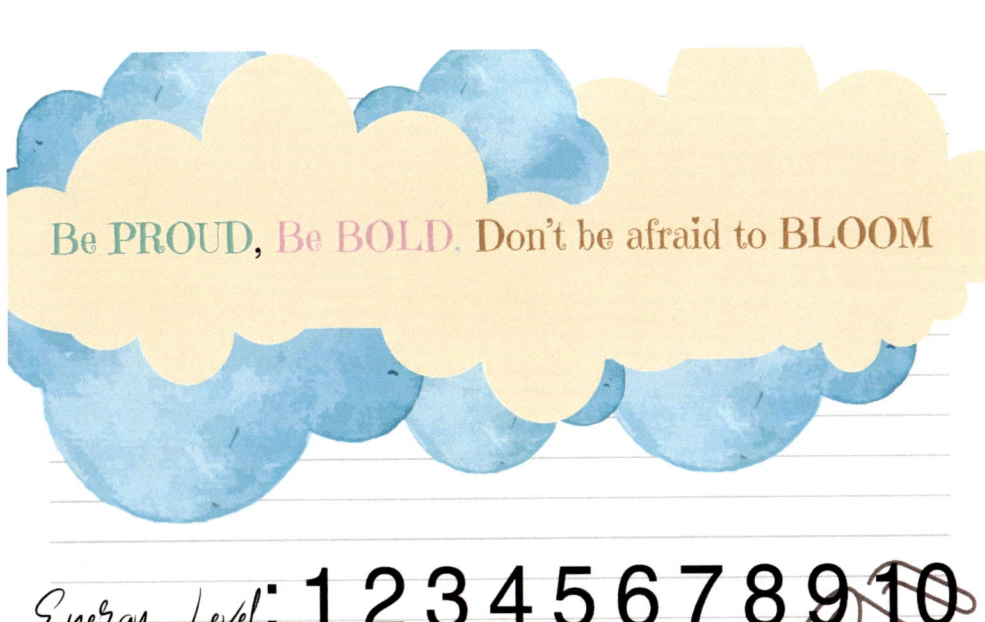

Energy Level: 1 2 3 4 5 6 7 8 9 10

Hydration Tracker:

Exercise

Today's physical Activity:

Minutes:

NOTES

This Weeks Affirmations:

Tomorrow's Focus

Beginning of Day
Thoughts

Time:

End of Day

Thoughts

Time:

DATE:

Today's **MOOD is:** 🙂 😊 😄 😣 😭 😓 😖

i am:
- ◯
- ◯
- ◯

My 6 Self Care Moments:

Breakfast:

Lunch:

Dinner:

Be PROUD, Be BOLD, Don't be afraid to BLOOM

Energy Level: 1 2 3 4 5 6 7 8 9 10

Hydration Tracker:

Exercise

Today's physical Activity:

Minutes:

NOTES

This Weeks Affirmations:

Tomorrow's Focus

Beginning of Day
Thoughts

Time:

End of Day

Thoughts

Time:

DATE:

Today's **MOOD** is: 😐 🙂 😄 😖 😭 😒 ☹

i am:
○
○
○

My 6 Self Care Moments:

Breakfast:

Lunch:

Dinner:

Be PROUD, Be BOLD. Don't be afraid to BLOOM

Energy Level: 1 2 3 4 5 6 7 8 9 10

Hydration Tracker:

Exercise

Today's physical Activity:

Minutes:

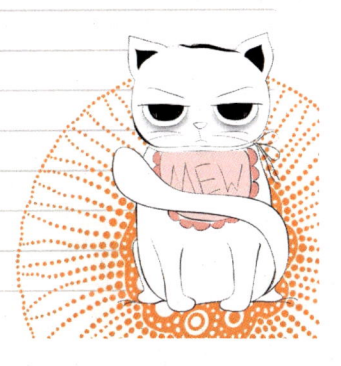

NOTES

This Weeks Affirmations:

Tomorrow's Focus

Beginning of Day
Thoughts

Time:

End of Day

Thoughts

Time:

DATE:

Today's **MOOD is:** 😐 🙂 😄 😖 😭 😒 😫

i am:
- ○
- ○
- ○

My 6 Self Care Moments:

Breakfast:

Lunch:

Dinner:

Be PROUD, Be BOLD, Don't be afraid to BLOOM

Energy Level: 1 2 3 4 5 6 7 8 9 10

Hydration Tracker:

Exercise

Today's physical Activity:

Minutes:

NOTES

This Weeks Affirmations:

Tomorrow's Focus

Beginning of Day
Thoughts

Time:

End of Day

Thoughts

Time:

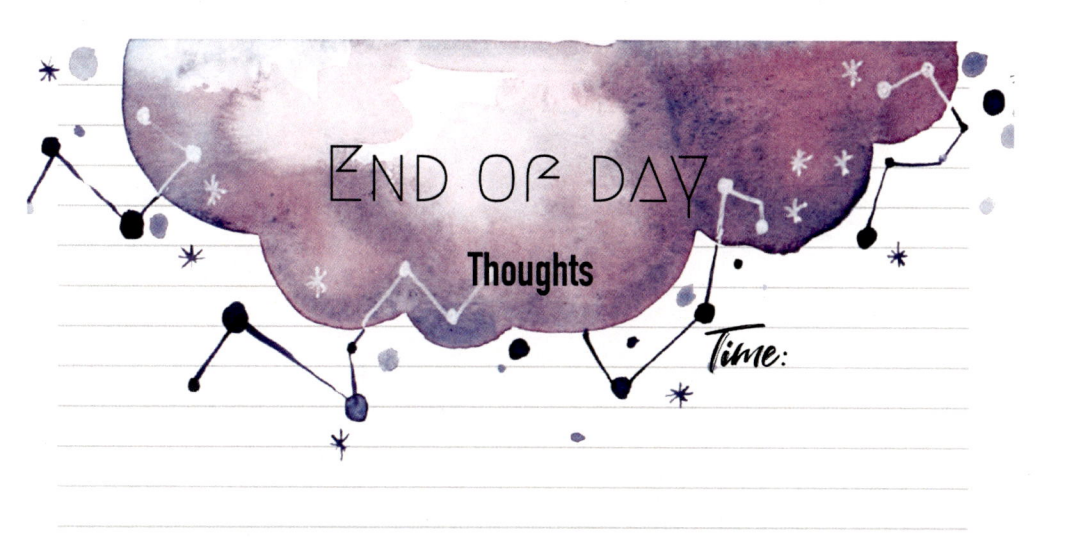

be PROUD
be BOLD
Don't be afraid
to
BLOOM

- Fiers Femme

Made in the USA
Columbia, SC
07 January 2023